I Fell in Love with His Promises

KAMA BURTON

ISBN: 978-0-9977942-2-9

DEDICATION

At one time, I didn't think I had anyone in my corner, not even the Lord. I felt alone, by myself and that no one cared for me. It seemed as if God left me alone and told me to do it myself, but I found that it was not true. I want first to say Thank you to my Lord and Savior Jesus Christ for allowing me to go through everything I've been through and bringing me out as He always has. I thank Him for being true to His words, which are His promises.

ACKNOWLEDGMENT

Thank you to my parents Ivory and Joyce Thomas for the continued support and unconditional love they have shown me all my life. The Lord gave me the best-SAVED parents in the world! I couldn't imagine not having them in my life. To my children, Clifford (Tha barber) I am so proud of you and your accomplishments. Cheyenne, my baby girl, my favorite girl, my twin; I am grateful to have you and so excited about your leadership skills and what God has for you. Cristopher, my baby boy, my "whomps", my skateboarder that has a drive that is out of this world, I push every single day to ensure you all have all you need. Not just financially, but spiritually as well. You are all my heartbeat—the reason I must stay focused and on the right path. My goal is to continue to show them that they can do all things through Christ that strengthens them. To my brothers Kilan and Chaka and Ivory Jr, thank you for always being there for me. Special thanks to my auntie Vanessa Moore for always being real with me and always thinking family first. I love you all! There is nothing like having friends that will support everything that you touch. To my best friend, DeAngela Sanders who has supported me along the way when I needed an ear to hear, a shoulder to cry on, or a prayer to get through because I was too weak to pray—I appreciate you. To Sonia Baldwin, my REALTOR sister, and my friend, thank you. You have been with me through all my down times and good times, and you are still here. Thank you, Connie Saunders, for just being a friend. You were the only person, at one time, to even know the reality of what I was going through. You were the very first person I called when I knew I had enough of my past.

Thank you to my riders, my friends, Rena Burton, LaKrecia Graham, and Cheryl Nichols. When I'm in need you are my girls to the rescue, thank you! The times we spend are priceless, and it means the world to me. To Dr. Harris and Shatam Odom, I thank you for continuing to believe in my dreams and supporting them. Lastly, I must say thank you to the two people that are very special to me. LaKecia "Muffin" Allen, your support, love, and realness keeps me focused on wanting to continue to be a mentor and an example. Antwan Demarco, I thank you for being a great friend and believing in me when everyone else said NO. You see something in me, which contributed to me getting out of my shell and pushing forward with all that my heart desire. I thank you, sir!

Bishop and Pastor John W. Thomas, of House of Prayer Reformation Church has been a real and genuine example of an overseer. You have been such a huge help to my family through difficult times. Bishop, you often tell me you are praying for my family and I. You're consistently checking on me and reminding me that things will be better. THANK YOU

CONTENTS

1 INTRODUCTION

It's funny how many times we fall in love with people. Not because of their physical appearance, but because of words they say to us and the excellent treatment that comes along with it—in the beginning at least. We as women are emotional. We love with our hearts and souls. For me, being in love is what I want to achieve. There is nothing like being in love with someone that loves you back the same way or even more. It should be a two-way street—a partnership. The problem is, when I fell in love (twice in my life) it always felt like a one-way street. One would say, "I love you" and treat me like crap. The other would say "I love you," but his actions didn't speak as loud as his words. It seems in both instances I was more of the aggressor of love and they loved what I was giving, but only for so long. No, I'm not talking about sex. I am referring to how I showed how much I cared through my actions. Being that listening ear, committing myself to them, and always telling them how I felt about them.

I am starting to believe; no one should use the word "LOVE" unless it is something that is mutually shown through actions. For example, love is an action, not just a word to be thrown around just because it's the thing to say or because you think you are feeling something.

How does Kama see love?

Love is a man wanting to take time to know me. Not just what I like to do, but who I am. He finds interest in what I do. He shows me this by supporting my business, my goals, and my vision. He has no problem being real with me when I mess up; without yelling, cussing me out, or talking down as if I have no feelings at all. He always finds me attractive by telling me consistently and not only at the beginning of our courtship. He wants to spend time with me by having fun and not being stuck doing the same things repeatedly.

It's imperative that he finds interest in my children, no matter their age, and it's genuine. It's not just because he wants to be with me. My children will tell me if it's real or a front. He would find interest in their lives and get to know them just as he wants to get to know me. He would start spending time with them because he wants to be that figure in their lives and the male support they need as they continue through this journey of life. He supports them in their activities and cares about them as if they were his own.

Most importantly, he is in love with my God, my Lord, and Savior. He prays with me and understands and respects my beliefs, because we are equally yoked. We can speak the word of God together, fellowship, and worship God together. We take time to fast as a couple and ask God for direction in our union. That is what love looks like to me.

2 GROWING UP

Kama, my first name, meaning inner love and beauty. Lynne, my middle name, derived from the name Linda, after my aunt whose life was brutally taken in the act of domestic violence via a murder/suicide. I was born, October 24, 1977, in beautiful Southern California and grew up in Inglewood, California, until I was 13 years old and moved to Hawthorne, California. My memories are overall great ones. I feel blessed to be raised by both my parents in the same household. Even today, when I go to their home, I smile knowing that they are still together. My mother was a powerful, no-nonsense parent. She always thought things out before making decisions about her children. My dad, a very hard-working man, always took excellent care of his children; my hero, my heart, and to this day, I am "daddy's

4

girl." I grew up with two brothers and myself in the household. I have one brother from another mother and one sister, Trina Latonya Thomas (God rest her soul) that I spent little time with, but they were always in my heart. One day, at age five, my mom was walking down the streets of Inglewood, looking for a church home. She was on Centinela Avenue about two blocks west of La Brea where she came across this little church sitting a little ways back from the street. It was a two-story building with the sanctuary at the top, and an area downstairs where they had a baptismal pool and where Sunday School was held. There was a very determined, dogmatic, man of God. One day in October 1982, my mom walked into that church and never looked back. My mother has been and still is a God-fearing woman. She wanted change in her life, and God led her to a church that would change her life forever. A few years later, my little brother Kilan witnessed to my dad and the church was moved to 1003 S. Prairie Ave Inglewood, California. My brother had to be no more than six or seven years old, and my father came to the church where he was Baptized in Jesus' name and filled with the Holy Ghost according to the book of Acts.

At age seven, my pastor baptized me in the name of Jesus, and a year later, I was filled with the gift of the Holy Ghost, with the evidence of speaking in tongues. The church was my life as a child. If the church doors were opened, Kama had to be there. I wanted to be at every service and anything else the church allowed us to be a part of. I met so many other young people; we had bonds like no other. My friends and I were very active in the church. Sister Howard was our Bible Bowl coach, who helped us compete in Bible bowl tournaments. We would take scriptures and learn everything about them. We had to learn every single word for the fill in the blank questions; we had to recite anywhere from one passage to several passages at a time, it was a great way to learn the word and have fun at the same time.

I remember being on Prairie and the church began to multiply. So much so that the men had to stand up around the walls and the children were asked to go to children's church in a large room in another part of the church. I recall several times my mother would not allow me to go, because she wanted her children in church with her. I wasn't allowed to sit with my friends during church as my mother wanted us to be focused on the word of God. I remember sometimes being in tears because she wouldn't allow me to sit with my friends. I thought my mom was the meanest mother in the WORLD! How dare she not let me sit with my friends and my friends' mothers didn't care! I thought she didn't t love me as their parents loved them, she just wanted to be mean. I later realized how all that worked out for my good. After church, my friend Sidra would ask me to go to her house. My mother would allow me to go occasionally, but not all the time. I recall a day when Sidra said, I talk to your dad, and he said you could come over. We told my mom, and she said NO! See, my mom was that mom that didn't allow us to spend the night everywhere or always be in people's house. The times she would let me go to Sidra's home, we had night service as well, and people would either go to someone's house after church or go out to dinner. My mom would tell me, "don't warm out your welcome." What's funny, once mom says no, dad had no say so. My dad would let me do what I wanted if he could help it, but it was the "enforcer," my mother that made the final decision about my whereabouts. My mom, although strict, is a sage woman. I always say, "if I just would have listened."

As a young girl in church, we went to conventions and council meetings where we met other young people. I recall my friends and I getting our hair freshly done, parents buying us new dresses and us being FLY at those conventions, so we thought. At the conventions, I packed clothes to change no less than three times a day. I had my outfit for "mid-day sessions and services", had to be cute at night service and arrive a little late so people can see how cute we were, and we always went to eat or hang out after service, so I had to change and NOT be in the same outfit I had on earlier that day, but that was me — always trying to be cute to get some cute boys' attention.

At one of the councils I met this guy, let's call him "J." J was a very handsome young man, I must say! All the girls liked him. I remember being at this hotel in Ontario, California called Red Lion, and I walked past him. All I could see was his cute, bright smile when he called me over there to speak to him. We exchanged numbers, and we began to talk. Eventually, we made it official and became a couple. I recall during that time; there was a girl, his ex-girlfriend from years prior when they were much younger, did not like me and turned her friends against me because he didn't want her, and he wanted me. It was the stupidest thing in the world. The sad thing is, many people are still dealing with this craziness today. He wants me, not her. She doesn't know me, but she can't stand me. It just doesn't sound right. One day we were at a hotel and as I was getting on the elevator to go to my room at a church convention, I heard her talking mess about me as she always did. At this point, I was fed up. I jumped off the elevator and let her know if she wants to fight me, let's go. I was so tired of her mouth! She had even told people that I had sex with her cousin, and I hadn't had sex with anyone! She started to spread lies and rumors, and at that point, I thought I would knock her head off her shoulder (so to speak). We were about 16 years old at this time, and I was fed up! Of course, she backed out and said she didn't say anything, but I didn't care where we were. I just wanted to beat her up at that point. This was a sign that I should've been obedient to my mother.

Growing up in the church, I continued to meet other people. We were taught never to be "unequally yoked with unbelievers." This means you don't date outside of the church. Not the visible church you are in specifically, but the body of Christ. So do not date those that don't believe the way you do. How can two walks together except they agree.

My mom didn't allow me to have a boyfriend until I was 16 years old, today I feel like that is still too young. My mother didn't want me to be introduced to anyone. In 9th grade, my friend called me and told me that she had two boys that wanted to talk to me. She was dating their friend, and they told her to hook them up with someone. She told me about them, and I was excited that I had a choice. As a young girl, not to sound conceited, but getting a boy was never a problem. Guys would always talk to me, and I always had a boyfriend (don't tell my mothe), it was before I was 16. I quickly learned, as my mom would say, "obedience is better than sacrifice."

3 WHEN HE CAME INTO MY LIFE

My friend gave me two numbers, and I didn't call either one. Finally, one day, I gave my friend a picture of me from when I was a cheerleader. She showed my picture to Curtis, and he told her that he had to talk to me. At that point, his interest had me feeling good and I chose to talk to him. We spoke over the phone a couple of times, and he asked if he could come out to see me. I, of course, said yes. I remember that day like it was yesterday. I wore all purple because it was my favorite color. I had on a purple shirt with purple pants and purple vans. When it was cold that evening, I put on a purple jacket. I remember my heart beating as if it was going to pop out of my chest, because of my nerves. I continued to stare out the window on the 2nd floor in my apartment building. Finally, he pulled up in a brown minivan that his mom dropped him off in.

I recall him walking up and knocking on the door. The first thing he said to me was "You look better in your picture" and began to laugh. It broke the ice very quickly, and we laughed about it. That night we sat outside under the steps and talked to get to know each other better. It just felt right. I was only 14, a freshman in high school, and he was 15, a sophomore in high school. I thought it was so cool to have a guy a little older than me.

Sometimes as young girls and honestly, as adults, we don't pay attention to the little details and signs. I recall my friend telling me that he smoked cigarettes, but I didn't care. She said he was fit; he worked out and was in good shape. I looked past the cigarettes and whatever else he was doing because I thought he was very good looking, and we clicked. The first night he left my house he asked me, "Will you be my girlfriend?" With a HUGE smile on my face I said, "Yes." There was something about this guy that I knew was going to last.

The first time he told me he loved me we were together for approximately a month. I had a 9 pm curfew at the time to get off the phone (that's what our kids need today). As we were ending the call he said, "Good night, I LOVE YOU." With a huge smile on my face and my heart dropped to my stomach. Out of excitement, I said, "good night" and hung up the phone. I went to school the next day and told my friend LaShaun and asked her what I should say to him. I was afraid that if I didn't say it back he would "quit" me. That's the term we used instead of breaking up. She asked me if I loved him and I said, "I think I do," but it seemed too soon. A couple of times after our daily evening conversations I finally responded, "I love you too."

Curtis would come over often and I would (at times) go to his house. We would have so much fun together. This day, we were play fighting downstairs at my apartment, and my mom came out the door to check on me. I heard her voice in a tone I hadn't heard unless I was in trouble. She called me from the screen door and said, "KAMA, GET UP HERE NOW." My mother didn't yell much, but she had a stern way of saying things to me to let me know something was not right. She stated she was checking on me, and she said that she saw something that was not right in his eyes. She said he didn't look like he was playing; he looked as if it was getting serious. It was almost like a movie; she stopped that "play fight" just in the nick of time. I teach girls often NOT to "play fight" because you just might hit him the wrong way and it might not turn out as you anticipated. She asked me what was going on. I went on to explain that we were "just playing" and she said not to ever play in that manner. From that point on, we never play fought again. These are the signs that we don't see because it seems so innocent—at the time.

By October of the same year, 1992, we were getting along well. I would go to his house, and he would come over to mine. I met his family; he met mine. It just seemed like we had a great thing going. We didn't argue at all. For the most part, we had such a great, almost perfect relationship.

Knott's Scary Farm is one of the most popular places for teens to go in October. One day, a friend of mine called me and said, "Aren't you going with Curtis?" Meaning in a relationship, and I said "Yes." She proceeded to say, well he is here with some of us and he is going to Knott's with Shelly. I immediately thought it wasn't true. Not shortly after the call, he walks in the room where she was, and she said, "Curtis, I have Kama on the phone." All I heard him say was "all shoot," and she said he ran out of the room. My heart was instantly shattered into pieces.

I laid in my daybed and cried all night long. I had a very restless night and was hurt beyond words. We were getting along so well to find out he had someone else he was dealing with besides me. The next morning, which was Saturday, I did not want to get out of bed. I had never dealt with hurt like this from a guy ever. For one, I wasn't allowed to have a boyfriend until I was 16 years old. I continued to tell my mother that he was just a "friend." I believe my disobedience was the reason I was hurt in this "relationship."

We broke up because he said he wanted to be with her and not me. About nine months later, I saw him at a park, and we started talking again. By this time, he had a car; he was able to pick me up and see me. We talked for a few weeks and decided to give this relationship another try. One of our most significant issues that never turned into an argument, but the cause of us breaking up to make up was the fact that I was a virgin and did not want to have sex before marriage. To an extent he respected that, but he felt he needed a release. Although he grew up in church, he needed to be sexually satisfied, and I couldn't give him that satisfaction.

4 WHEN MY LIFE BEGAN

As a young girl, I knew I wanted to be a homemaker; it was my lifelong dream. I would still love to have that life. The Virtuous Woman (Proverbs 31 10-31) is a perfect example of where I would like to see myself headed when I have a husband. I would dream of seeing myself at home, cooking breakfast for my family, making lunch for my husband, and leaving notes in his lunch bag. Spending time at home raising my children until they were school aged, then taking them to school and volunteering and being there for all their events. As a family, I saw us going on vacation, eating dinner together, and having family time. Most importantly, I saw us praying and worshipping together as a family.

I remember, as a child, my mother had bible studies often with us at home. Although I would hang over the bed or lay on the side of the bed on the floor, twiddling my fingers and couldn't wait until it was over, I look back and see the seeds she planted, and I thank God for that foundation. I remember some nights we would pray as a family, my mother, father, and brothers. There was no question about it, we did it, and this is what I wanted as a family.

My mother always used to say, "Obedience is better than sacrifice," and she was RIGHT! At age 19, I knew my dreams had come true. I was going to be a bride. Another one of my heart's desires were to be married at a young age. I believed if a person was indeed in love, the age of marriage didn't matter, let's be honest, many married at 14 in the early 1900s. Why would this be different? (Those were my thoughts at the time.)

Growing up in church, I was taught that sex before marriage is a sin. It's called fornication, and I still believe that. The only problem is that we never really went into the consequences of fornication other than, you're going to hell if you do it. I was so afraid of hell; I kept myself as a virgin until the time I married. It was almost shameful to admit, but I got pregnant as a virgin, don't believe me, Google it! My mom would tell me what you do in the dark will come to light. She was RIGHT, once again. I would go to my then boyfriends house, and we would go into his room, which I know my parents would not have been pleased with. Most of the time, I would start off hanging out in his back room. His mom had added a back room and bedroom to the home, and once he became a certain age, he would use that for his area. After a date, we would go to his house late and use the back door many times not to disturb the house. My intentions were ALWAYS to stay in that back room, visible, but he would convince me to go into the room, and I would fall for it every single time.

As a young girl in love, I didn't want to disappoint my boyfriend because he might "quit me." I wanted to please him more than I wanted to please my mother. On this day, we were in his room messing around, and he tried to have sex with me. I remember we didn't have clothes on from the waist down. I am a VERY private person when it comes to my body, so it was not easy to even get that far. At this time, he tried to penetrate, and my spirit didn't feel right. I was like we can't do this. He kept saying, that's okay, you're just scared. After enough of me saying I didn't want to do it, we stopped, and put our clothes back on. We went to a Chinese food restaurant that I loved, we had lunch, and I dropped him off at work. I knew he was mad to get that far and still NOTHING. I didn't think anything of it. I continued to go on about my day.

About a month later, my period didn't come. I was wondering what was happening because we didn't go all the way. I remember just hearing, about a year earlier, how another girl that I knew growing up in church ended up getting pregnant as a virgin. I recall my friends and I questioning did this happen? We couldn't believe it! But then it happened to me. We went to the drug store in Ladera Heights hoping no one would notice us purchasing a pregnancy test, and the test showed up "positive." I didn't know how to feel; I was numb. All I remember doing was looking in the mirror and saying, "Kama, you are pregnant." The first people I told were two close friends from church, but I couldn't tell my mother and father—it would devastate them.

At this time, he and I were broken up after the "almost" sexual encounter. We would break up on and off for five years because I wouldn't have sex with him; it was the strangest relationship. I remember his mom felt we should be married. She and I had an excellent relationship, and I still love her to this day. On the other hand, my parents, well, let's say it was the toughest thing I had to ever tell them. I remember letting my mother know that I was pregnant. All I remember was silence and the look of hurt and disappointment in her face. I know I had not only hurt her, but possibly embarrassed her. My mother is a powerful, devoted woman of God. She raised us in church and has always been a great example of a real saved, Christian woman. She was devastated by the news and didn't speak to me for three days. My dad, on the other hand, was very hurt, and he did express that to me. However, he said, "There is nothing we can do at this point." I know my dad was disappointed in me, but he said, "We all make mistakes". I had a bit of relief hearing this from my father.

Once she began to speak to me, she told me that I wasn't allowed to see him again. By this time, she didn't know I had already made up in my mind that we were getting married. It was tough to reveal that information to her. She doesn't want me to see him and now I have to say, "Hey mom, here's your new son in law?!?"

I believe it's essential that we listen to our parents. Many of you reading this at this moment are adults and can recall times that we were told not to do something, and we did it anyway, at the same time reaping the consequences of our actions. My mother was seeing things that I never paid attention to. After hearing this news of my pregnancy, my life would change forever.

5 THE MARRIAGE

On April 10, 1997, we married. The day of the short ceremony with myself, my then-husband, the minister and her son that continued to peak his head in and out of the chapel, my mom was ANGRY and said she would NOT support what I was doing when I told her this was the day I was getting married. She later walked out the door with anger and said, "I DON'T CARE WHAT YOU DO!!" I remember feeling hurt, but my mind was made up. Before we went to get married, my aunt called. She told me that my mom was there and if I wanted her (my mom) to come with me to get married, she would come. I declined. At this point, I didn't want anyone to be a part of this ceremony. I just wanted to get married and move on with life.

After the ceremony, I went home to pack some of my clothing to head to my new address. When I came home, my mom had purchased me some lingerie and some new "unmentionables." It was almost as if all the emotions she had went away. By this time, my dad was cool with my decision, but we know that men don't show their emotions as women do.

6 THIS WAS JUST THE BEGINNING

April 11th, 1997, we went to the movies in El Segundo. I remember walking to the car and not feeling right on the inside. We sat in the car, and I had an emotional breakdown. I told him, "I can't do this!" and cried. He began to laugh and say, "you're just scared." I recall thinking in my head "I'm not scared; I know I just made the biggest mistake of my life."

We were living with his mom for the first few months of our marriage. They couldn't seem to get along at all. He was quite disrespectful to her. One day he called her out of her name, and she had enough. I remember her telling me, "It's not you, but he has to go!" She was fed up and tired. Tired of the disrespect, because that wasn't the first time he was disrespectful towards her. As a young wife, I didn't see that this would eventually trickle down to me. Before our marriage, we had a conversation. He said he didn't want to be like his dad, which was a cheater and abusive. He promised me that he would never put his hands on me. He was going to love me the right way. During the five years of our "off and on" relationship, I didn't pay attention to the signs of his abusive behavior that would later be a part of my story.

In high school he slapped a girl (that wasn't his girlfriend), because she made him upset and got in his face. I figured it wasn't "me" and it wasn't a "girlfriend." He had more respect for me as a girlfriend. At the same time, he did cheat on me before that with the girl at Knott's Scary Farm. But we were young and dumb, which means he got a pass for that. Warning sign after warning sign, but I had my love blind shades on.

Before we (and I say we because, at this point, he was my husband) were kicked out of the home, who he really was came out so clearly. In the 90's we were using Pagers. If you had a cell phone, that means you either stole it or was balling' out of control, because they were not cheap at all. I continued my church habits. Sunday morning church, Sunday night service, and Wednesday night Bible study. This Sunday, he was paging me several times to call him. I remember looking at my phone and saying, I don't want to be there and questioning myself. I decided not to return his call and told myself I would talk to him when I get home. I got home somewhere between 10:45 pm and 11:00 pm. My friends and I were talking as we always do. There used to be a time we would stay until midnight. My dad had started the BOLD ministry, which was the security of our church and pastor. That meant, sometimes we didn't leave until everyone was gone. That gave me time to spend with my friends, because we didn't see each other during the week.

When I arrived at home, he was HOT!!! He was agitated, asking me why I didn't answer his calls. There was nothing I could say, because I honestly didn't want to answer the question. He said, "Since you don't know how to respond, you can only go to church on Sunday mornings and anything at night is OUT! On top of that, you now have a 10 pm curfew!" All I could do is cry and ask why? He responded that since I am a wife now, the things I use to do, I couldn't do anymore. He also went on to say that my parents had me on a 10 pm curfew and he was going to stick to that because I was used to it. Nineteen years old, married, and almost a mother and I had a curfew, not to mention 10 pm. He had to forget all the times that my parents allowed me to come home later if they knew where I was. Most of the movies we went to didn't start until after 9 pm, and with the type of work he had, he would rarely get off before 7 pm, especially on a Friday and Saturday. I would try to argue that, but of course, I always lost the argument because to him, I was still wrong.

After we moved, it was time for us to purchase furniture for the house. I had pretty good credit at the time, and we had decided to check out Levitz furniture store. We found a cute set we wanted to purchase. I asked him if he was sure that he could make the payment because I would be going out on maternity leave for a while and didn't know when I was returning to work. He assured me that he would make the payment. After leaving Levitz, we went down the street to Circuit City. He said he just wanted to look at the PlayStation™ and possibly purchase the console and no more than two games. Four to five games later, I walked out with ANOTHER monthly payment and a promise that he would take care of the bill.

In the back of my mind, I knew we couldn't make the payment. He didn't care, he got what he wanted, and he was happy. Since he was pleased, and I didn't have a say, I made myself feel happy. The stores always have a gimmick. Buy now and no payments for 3 or 6 months; however, (months later) the bills are coming due. He decides, since he doesn't have the money (which I'm almost sure he did) he wasn't paying. The anxiety that went through my body had me feeling as if I was going to explode. He refused to pay the bills. The next bill came—he didn't pay that bill either. It began to be a reason each month as to why he didn't pay the bill, and at times, he didn't allow me to pay them either. The control he had over me was insane.

As time went on, I would bug him about going out more, spending more time together, more family time, and hanging out with our friends. I would remind him of those promises that were promised to me. I did not want to let go of our marriage unless these promises did not come to pass. I felt in my heart, if he followed through with what he said, we would be happy, and our marriage could have lasted.

Throughout the marriage, the control turned in to various types of abuse. Physical, verbal, emotional, sexual, and financial. He made me feel as if I was the worse person on the face of the earth at times. I would question myself, why did I marry him? Better yet, why did he marry me? Was it out of convenience? You know they say, "it's cheaper to keep her." I never thought in a trillion years I would have a story to tell about domestic violence, let alone go around telling my story. But when you fall into this thing called "Love" it seems like anything is bound to happen. One day, towards the official end of our communication, a couple of years after the divorce, he finally admitted, he did things to manipulate me, because he said he knew what would get to me. He knew what would push my buttons and get me to do just about anything for him. He made broken promises and lied to me to break me, but thank God I was able to move forward, because some women live with this type of behavior their entire lives.

7 THE ONE, SO I THOUGHT

Later, I began dating someone that I was really "digging." He was such a great guy that for a minute, I just knew he was "the ONE." I would fantasize about us being out on dates holding hands, laughing, and having deep conversations that lasted for hours. I would see us together at different events and always would imagine him sitting in the audience, front and center as I went out to speak at various events. He would sit there with that cute smile of his, proud that HIS woman was up there doing what she does.

I ended up falling in love with a man that I felt was my "Prince Charming," my "Knight in shining armor." He came to rescue me from the hurt and hell I had gone through in my previous marriage. I found myself falling for him WAY to quickly. He called me daily and sometimes we texted throughout the day. We had very similar ways of thinking as well as things in common. I was fascinated by him. Mainly because he found interest in me, and I never had to adjust who I was for him. He loved me because I was different. I remember when he first told me he was falling in love with me. I died (so I thought) but then came back to life quickly. Someone could fall in love with me, knowing my past? Knowing that I was in a very controlling abusive marriage that made me feel like I was a weak woman, he saw my strength and loved my drive. He was tall, dark, and handsome just like I like them—well the dark and handsome part. He had it going on for the most part.

He was making decent money, drove a nice car, and was one of the most respectful and patient men I had ever met. Not that I had met many in my life, but he was and still is a good guy. As time went on things changed in his life, and it made it hard for me. I didn't care how much money he had, because I have never been about material things. All that mattered to me was that he cared about my children and me. Now don't get me wrong, I'm not settling for anyone. But life happens, and sometimes we must deal with the cards we were dealt.

Being with him made me happy. To hear his voice or see his name on my text messages made me feel so good inside. I don't know if anyone ever felt like I did, but I was always in awe that someone had me, Kama, on their mind. While we were talking, there was no one else that could come to me to tear me away from him. I don't care how fine Idris Alba is, or how much I was in love with Ice Cube (night and day right lol), but this man was the only one that could have my heart. He understood me and didn't feel like he had to disrespect me to tell me how he felt. Who does that without yelling or cursing someone out these days? I was used to that in my previous marriage. My ex-husband would tell me how he felt, but it was sometimes after a bad fight or while he was drinking.

As time went on, I found myself falling deeper and deeper in love. I remember him telling me how he saw us walking down the aisle getting married. Even in my old age (lol) of 33 at the time, why wouldn't I still be in love with the idea of being in love? Does this feeling ever really die in a woman? He told me how he would never put his hands on me in an abusive way. We discussed having fun and going out. I would dream of going to the beach with him, and we would chill as we watch the sunset together. It's the small things that matter to me. When we may be low on funds, we can have a picnic at the park. I would fantasize about the simplest things in life that would make us happy. At the same time, we can get to know one another and enjoy everything about life.

Unfortunately, we didn't work out. After one conversation that I dreaded to have because of the decision I had to make, "WE" weren't the same. The sad thing is, I knew this was coming before it came to pass. The best thing is, I had prepared myself for this. Don't get me wrong, I saw this coming well in advance, but I held on to this for a long time. Although it doesn't take away from who he is (which I still believe to be a good man) it had me thinking about why I was so in love with him and couldn't shake this feeling.

After about a month and a half of me asking God to PLEASE remove the feelings I have for this guy, I was still trying to understand, why am I so in love? What is it about him that makes me feel as if I cannot shake this feeling? I later realized it's because I fell in love with his promises. Just let that sink in for a moment.

Begin to think back to someone one you fell in love with and still may be in love with them today, but that person doesn't love you back. You, just like me, had been trying to figure out "why am I in love still?" What is it about that person that makes my heart jump when I see their name? Why am I still awaiting that good morning text, and praying for that good night text? Why am I praying that I get flowers on the doorstep or a nice text to say you are all I want? As God revealed to me, I fell in love with his promises, man's promise.

Being a devoted Christian wanting to serve God the best way I know how, I thought to myself, if I fell in love with his promises and stayed as committed as I am, I needed to fall deeper in love with God's promises. His promises will come to pass. 1st Corinthians 1:20 "For all the promises of God in him are yea and in him Amen, unto the glory of God by us." This tells me that once God says it, IT, whatever IT is, shall be and will be done. There is no reason for me to be scared, nervous, or doubtful because the God I serve will take care of me in every aspect of my life.

As women, we seek after love. No matter how hard we try to go around it, it is part of the "curse." Curse? What Curse? Do you know the story about Adam and Eve? When they were in the Garden of Eden and Eve decided she wanted to eat of the forbidden tree. You know how it is when you are fasting, and it seems all the good food is making a debut in your eyesight? Your office has decided to do a potluck, or someone decides to bring in your favorite pastry that you've been asking about for months, and the person keeps saying soon, and the day you fast is THE day. In your mind, the first thing you say is "Well, I'll eat this "one meal" today and fast for the rest." You become anxious, and you end up breaking your fast and messing up on your blessing just because you had to have that ONE MEAL. That's what happened to Eve. She allowed the serpent (enemy) to convince her that eating of the "Tree of life" was okay, because God was trying to hide something from them. One of the first promises of God was, if they ate of this tree that was amid the Garden, they would surely die (Genesis 3:3). We know how that ended; she ate of the tree after convincing Adam to do the same. God made another promise to Eve and stated, "Unto the woman he said, I will greatly multiply thy sorrow and thy conception: in sorrow, thou shalt bring forth children, and thy desire shall be to thy husband, and he shall rule over thee" (Genesis 3:16). Ladies, we were put on earth to be a man's helpmate (Genesis 2:18).

Therefore, I believe we fall in love so quickly with his words or his current actions. What do I mean by current actions? Current actions are the ways we are being treated at that moment. Sometimes we are in "the moment" and that moment feels good and we don't want to let go, though everything around us still isn't right. When things begin to change, we hold on to what we felt and pray to God that this would stay the same.

This reminds me of someone that is addicted to drugs. I've asked why would someone be addicted to drugs, and what is it about that drug that they know is not good for their bodies? Most of the time, I heard they want that high and feeling they had from the first "hit." Although I've never done drugs, I understand that they never experience that feeling again and that's what keeps them addicted. Yes, they still get high, but that feeling is not the same from the first feeling. It reminds me of the first kiss, the first touch of a man. You want it more and more, and this is what draws you closer to him. If it was good, you can't seem to take your hands off each other (in a good way), until something happens in the relationship such as a bad argument or disagreement.

Ladies, we were created to be a man's helpmate. No matter how hard we try to fight it, it is what it is. No women's liberation can change that; it's just part of who we are. Therefore, we fall in love with a man and get so emotionally tied to him. He is to be the head of the household, NOT master, but our head, meaning that it's up to him to have the final say on some things with guidance from the Lord. Don't get me wrong, that doesn't mean that what you say doesn't matter, but I'm sure I've lost a few of you already, thinking "Girl please, he ain't running nothing over here!" Well, let me ask you this question: are you in a relationship? Are you happy? Is HE happy? Be real with yourself. Ladies, we must check ourselves first. Being the head of your household means that he is following what God says and leading you the correct way. When we put God in our relationships/marriages, we can't go astray, because he hears clearly from the Lord. Don't be afraid of the words "head of household." Communication is key, and with clear and proper communication, your relationships can be great. Just like having clear and proper communication with the Lord, if we follow what HE tells us to do, all things will work for our good. We can't be like Adam and Eve and continue to be disobedient when the Lord gave us specific orders. Remember this, "God is not a man, that he should lie; neither the son of man, that he should repent: hath he said, and shall he not do it? Or hath he spoken, and shall he not make it good?" (Numbers 23:19)

Now let's discuss "man." This entire subject is a never-ending story. Not in just a bad way, but a good way as well. I love a good dark, tall (my new preference, but whatever the Lord says, lol), strong, handsome man. Let's be real ladies; we tend to fall for a man that has a little swag, can dress, and know what to say to us. But no matter how fine and sexy he may look on the outside, we need to look on the inside and see if that is a great fit for us. Many people love chocolate, the candy not a man, but we don't always know what's inside. Have you ever received a box of assorted candy and didn't know what was on the inside? However, it looked so good that you tried one, and it was NOT what you expected? That's what you get when you meet someone new. Yes, a man can look all good and sexy on the outside; however, on the inside, he may be ugly due to his bad attitude or the way that he treats you. Many times, it can be that a person is nice within, but not the one for you.

Let's say you find a man that you are interested in. After a few dates and great conversation, you are ready to move forward into a relationship. It seems like the dating period was perfect, he would pick you up on time, brought you flowers, took you places you have never been, called you and text you more often than you are used to from a man. He begins to say, "when you're my lady we'll do…. when you're my woman; I'm going to take you…" We've heard it all before. Promise after promise and what happens, we tend to fall in love with his promises.

It's time for that to change.

Being the woman that I am, falling in love, is my lifelong dream. However, I look forward to being in love with someone that loves me back even more so. I love the thought of love, and no one is ever going to change that feeling. I often hear many people say things such as, "I would never fall in love again," "There is no such thing as love," "Men are dogs and all men cheat," however, I beg to differ. There are some great men out there looking for a great woman. Think about this; we are probably only going to have ONE man in our life anyway unless your spouse passes away and you remarry. A friend of mine just mentioned to me how she heard that dating is to collect data. I agree that's what it is. I don't want to listen to the dreams you had about me or what you want to do with me. I need to know what you plan for yourself and how I possibly fit in that plan. I don't want us to be that square peg trying to fit into a round hole. I need to know that I fit in your life. But I'm sure many others feel the same way.

Falling in love is the easiest thing to do, but falling out of love is the hardest—I'm here to tell you! But what makes us fall in love, and how do we fall out of love? It is his promises that we tend to fall in love with. We visualize ourselves holding hands, being affectionate, hanging out with friends and family, and so much more. Many tend to forget the struggles of a relationship. We tend to forget that we need to learn who we are and how we deal with the trials that may hit the relationship. I know and hopefully, you know, there is no perfection in any relationship. Let's be real; we are suckers for love. However, we must not fall in love with the foolishness. I made up in my mind that no matter what happens, I don't want a man to tell me he loves me until he shows me. Words are one thing, but his actions are absolutely everything.

Patience is Key. "Know this, that the trying of your faith worketh patience. But let patience have her perfect work, that ye may be perfect and entire, wanting nothing (James 1:3-4)." This is one of my favorite scriptures because I know that everything good takes time. There is no such thing as an overnight success. It takes an average of 5 years before the goal you have been working hard to accomplish begins to flourish. In the meantime, you work on that goal consistently to achieve what's coming. It's time to focus on the promises of God and fall in love with HIS promises.

We must change who's promises we fall in love with. "For

all the promises of God in him are yea and in him Amen, unto the glory of God by us (2 Corinthians 1:20).

We often try to do things our way whenever God doesn't move in our time. We expect things to happen overnight and it just doesn't for 99.9% of the folks out there that God has promised them something.

In the next few chapters, you will learn how to look at God's promises and not man's promises.

We will focus on God's promises and his results, as well as, Man's promises, and his results. If we focus on what God wants us to do, many will find themselves with the man that God has for them.

8 I'M NOT GOING ANYWHERE (NEVER LEAVE YOU, NOR FORSAKE YOU)

There is nothing more soothing than knowing someone is always going to be there for and with you. It gives you a feeling of comfort, because you know that they will still be in your life. That promises tend to come up often. When there is a disagreement, when a person cheats on you or disrespects you, they come back and say, "I love you, and I'm not going anywhere," but the reality is they left you before the disrespect and in the midst of it. Maybe not just physically, but mentally as well. However, when God says I will never leave you nor forsake (abandon) you, He means what he says. He will not do anything to hurt you. Most situations that come upon us happens because of our own doing.

Many of us have felt and experienced abandonment at some time in our lives, whether it be from a parent leaving the household or losing someone in death. Most of us have experienced abandonment in a relationship and to get through it, it requires work and lots of it to get things back to where they used to be. However, we tend to worry about being in love and keeping someone rather than watching their actions to see if their tendencies show us who they are. I believe people show and tell us in an indirect way they are going to leave soon. By not only their words, but their actions. We choose not to see what is right before our eyes, because we don't want to live with the truth of feeling like we are abandoned.

Man will leave you high and dry and have you stuck trying to figure out what you've done wrong and many times; it may not be you. He could have easily lost interest, and you didn't pay attention to the signs early enough. Maybe something in his life was happening, and he didn't know how to handle it. Maybe he felt it was better to leave. Maybe he is used to others hurting him, and he made up in his mind that no one will "leave me before I leave them."

It could be a variety of reasons; however, his promises are

not always his bond.

Going through tough times in our lives, we feel like God is like a man where we feel a sense of abandonment, and we must remember that He, God hasn't abandoned us because He is NOT a man. It's imperative that we look at God as consistent and that He is still there through the good and bad. For example, it takes us to have a pocket full of money, happiness in our relationships, and our personal lives for us to feel like God is there. We think only if things are going very well, God is here. He must be, because I am living the life! However, when our lives begin to take a turn for what we feel is the worst, we swear God has abandoned us! He has forgotten about us; there is no way He is still here for us, because we have hit a roadblock in our lives.

God is ever so present in our life. I remember going through a hard time in my life, and I just knew God had left me. I couldn't seem to feel his presence no matter what I was going through. The feeling would intensify itself when I was going through the emotional part of the breakup and separation in my life. I couldn't understand how the Lord would let me continue to feel as I did. Because of that, I felt like he had given up on me due to the decisions that I made. It seemed like I had absolutely no hope. The thought of completely giving up on God because I thought He had given up on me would continually come across my mind. But for some reason, I guess it was the spirit of God that is within me, reminded me of God's promise, "I will never leave you nor forsake you." My mind began to change at the very moment. My doubt began to turn back into hope. I would remind myself of the Lord and His word, and immediately, I started to see change. My faith began to become stronger and stronger day by day.

As I reflect on my life and what I have been through, I am a believer that God will never leave me.

9 I WANT TO TREAT YOU LIKE YOU'VE NEVER BEEN TREATED

Think about a time you've been hurt. Whether from a family member, friend, or someone you were in a relationship with. The person made a promise to you and didn't follow through. I recall driving with my ex-husband before we were married discussing how he was going to treat me. He said he wasn't going to ever "put his hands on me." He said he didn't want to do what he had seen in the past and he was very clear about what was right and wrong.

On the other hand, he did the absolute opposite of what he said he would do. We had our times and our moments when things were going very well. We would be happy, and he would consider me and my feelings. It felt good to be treated like a woman and feel wanted. I fell deeper in love when his actions and his words lined up. Those were the promises I fell in love with.

It was my goal to ensure he treats me as a human being and a woman as he had done in the past. It's not like he doesn't know how or hadn't done it before. He wasn't foreign to it. Many people never understand how abused women stay with their abusers, but one of the reasons the victim stays or goes back is because they know what it feels like for him to be a kind and loving person momentarily as we discussed earlier. However, this temporary change has our minds focused on the potential and not the mental issues and insecurities that are right before us.

As I was pondering on what it's like to have a man treat me like the queen that I am, I began to think about the Lord. Thinking about how He (God) has treated me throughout my life despite my downfalls, disobedience, and sins. He still loves me and always forgives me of my downfalls. I never understand how it is I can do things I know are wrong and the Lord says, He is still here with me always (Matthew 28:20). My thoughts are that He (God) is a gentleman when I need doors open. He opens each door. He tells us to ask, and it shall be given, seek, and we shall find, knock, and the door shall be open (Matthew 7:7). If Jesus is telling us this, it means that we can stand on his word and believe that it will be done. He continues to treat us the way we should be treated.

No man or woman should be treated less than who they are. It should be a mandate that everyone treats others like they deserve to be treated. Although people call this the "Golden Rule," the Bible says, "And as ye would that men should do to you, do ye also to them likewise." (Luke 6:31).

Having a conversation with friends, we were discussing people's thoughts about submission and how one is to be treated in the marriage. People that feel as if abuse or mistreatment of their spouse is okay; they need to read God's word in its entirety. It's essential to get an understanding of what God is truly saying to the people.

Being in church, one of the things that bother me is when someone blames God for another man's misunderstanding of the scriptures. The Bible tells you, "in this same way; husbands ought to love their wives as their bodies. He who loves his wife loves himself. After all, no one ever hated their own body, but they feed and care for their body, just as Christ does the church." (Ephesians 5:28-29). Does that sound like it's okay for a man to treat his wife as if she is less than him? I don't think so. The bible says that the woman is the weaker vessel. "Likewise, ye husbands, dwell with *them* according to knowledge, giving honor unto the wife, as unto the weaker vessel, and as being heirs together of the grace of life; that your prayers be not hindered." (1 Peter 3:7). Being the weaker vessel doesn't mean you should treat her as if she doesn't exist. It means to be her strength, her protector, her lover!

As we continue to search the scriptures, we find how God's word teaches us how to treat everyone in our lives. We don't have to take revenge on anyone, because the word says, "Dearly beloved, avenge not yourselves, but *rather* give place unto wrath: for it is written, Vengeance *is* mine; I will repay, saith the Lord." (Romans 12:19). How can we not fall in love with a God that will protect you from the enemy and those that treat you wrong? We can't do half of what God can. I've learned to allow the Lord to fight my battles, because the battle is not mine. It's the Lord's.

Why do I Love praise and worship so much? It's because it's refreshing to sing praises to God and let him know how much I love him. I find myself often singing old songs I would hear at church growing up. One in particular, "I love you, Lord, and I lift my voice to worship you OH my soul rejoices. Take joy, my King in what you hear and let it be a sweet, sweet sound in Your ear!". It's something about singing to Him (God), and I genuinely believe that is where my strength comes. If you haven't tried it, please do so. It feels good to let the Lord know in song how you feel. David, in the Bible, wrote many chapters of Psalms that are songs to the Lord.

David encouraged himself in the Lord, which is something we all should do. When we do this, we find how the Lord will continue to treat us as we should be treated. I never understood how you fall in love with a person over and over again, but the more I study my word, attend church, pray and fast, I draw closer to Him (God), and I fall in love more and more. Try it. What talents can you give back to the Lord? Watch how he will continue to open doors for you and treat you like you deserve. The Bible says that we "reap what we sow" (Galatians 6:7). This scripture is a reminder for me to know, anyone that has treated me wrong; only God can take care of them. It's not my duty. Although I wanted to be the one to get revenge, there is no better way than to turn it over to the Lord I serve.

10 I LOVE YOU

Who does not LIVE to hear those three little words for the first time? I LOVE YOU! It puts a huge smile on my face just thinking about the next time I hear those words from a man that means it. But what does LOVE mean to you? Although I get excited when I hear this word LOVE, I've made up my mind; I can go without hearing it too soon in a relationship, because I believe the word LOVE is an action. There are a lot of actions that must take place behind that word.

Love will not lie to you. Love is gentle; love is kind. There was a song that one of the ministers at my former church, Peace Apostolic, sung. My friends and I LOVED this song. It goes, "Love is kind, it's kind all the time. Yes, it's true, because I love you." Love is kind, and love does not hurt. My ex-husband would tell me he loves me all the time. After a while, it was said so much the feeling I use to feel left. That warm and fuzzy feeling where my stomach would get butterflies moments after he would say it was all gone! The reason why? I didn't believe it.

Who could believe a person that says they love you in one breath and cuss you out or verbally abuse you in the next breath really loves you? But I must keep it real, for a while, I didn't believe he loved me unless he cussed me out or put his hands on me. The entire thought process began to get twisted. I remember a time when my ex-husband gave me the silent treatment, because he was so mad at me. I did everything I could to get him to hit me because I had it in my mind; he didn't love me unless he hits me. It was a very sick thought, but that was the way I had identified love with him. At least when he did that, I knew that he would speak to me afterward, and he would get whatever he was dealing with out of his system. It was a bad situation for me mentally.

I've learned love communicates clearly without harsh words. Love says, "honey; I'm not ok with what you said or did." Love informs. When someone truly loves you, they will protect you from anything that will harm you, including themselves. They would walk away, leave for a few hours to cool down, or even express how they feel without demeaning you. Therefore, the Love of Christ is like no other. The word of God says in Ephesians 5:25, "Husbands, love your wives, even as Christ also loved the church, and gave himself for it." When we wait for the man that God has called us to be with, LADIES, we will experience a love like no other.

Sometimes I sit and think, "Lord, why me?" How could you love me after all my disobedience? How can you continue to bless me? Why did you die on the cross for my sins? You didn't have to do it, but you did! John 3:16, "For God so loved the world, He gave his ONLY begotten son, that whosoever believeth in Him should not perish but have everlasting life." Jesus gave His life for you and me. I never understood how people turned their backs on the Lord as if He did something wrong to them. It was your sins that had him on Calvary. God said, I will never leave you nor forsake you. Yet, and still we blame God when everything is going to the left, while praising him when things are going right. I feel it's unconditional love on the part of those that do this, but we sometimes don't realize or want to admit we brought this on ourselves.

1 Corinthians 13:4-8 "Love is patient. Love is kind; it does not envy; it does not boast; it is not proud. It does not dishonor others; it is not self-seeking; it is not easily angered; it keeps no record of wrongs. Love does not delight in evil but rejoices with the truth. It always protects, always trust, always hopes always perseveres. Love never fails…."

Take a moment and think about all the times you went through a difficult time, and you called on the Lord, and He answered. Think about how He continues to take care of your situation repeatedly during it all—even in our disobedience. He still loves us. Hebrews 12:6, "For whom the Lord loveth he chastened and scourged every son whom he receives." When you have been out of the will of God and you "reap what you sow," know that God is just trying to let you know, He still loves you, but you are going to go through a few things.

There is no greater love than what one can experience

through Christ. Throughout the word of God, He took care of those He loved because He knows that we can do greater in life. We will make mistakes and sometimes even rebel, but the Love of Christ never fails, and he stays with us always. Jesus said, "…. lo, I am with you always, even unto the end of the world." If you take the time to meditate on those words, you should examine the person in your life. Are you dealing with being angry or proud? Are we dishonoring him/her? Are you not trusting? Ask the Lord to renew your heart and theirs. There is no reason to be with someone you don't love or doesn't love you. At the same time, God can restore anything, if you believe and if it's in His will.

11 I WANT TO TAKE CARE OF YOU

As a man, well as far as the ones I know, it's essential for them to be secure in their employment for them to take care of their families. I remember having a conversation with a gentleman, and he said one thing about a real man is that he wants to "protect and provide" for his woman. Sometimes I'm amazed at the lack of protection and how much I ended up providing more for my family than he ever really did.

I remember being in the first home my ex-husband and I lived in, in Riverside, California. Our goal was to purchase the house from the owner eventually. It was going to be our 1st home to buy together. One day we began to get into an argument, or should I say, he yelled, and I begged (but I'll leave that part for another book). He was so upset about something very minor (well at least to me) that he said "from this point on, you pay ALL the bills, and I am not paying for anything." I was in AWE! He can not be serious! I'm his wife, and he is the father of my children. This must be a joke. As time went on, I found that he was not joking. He would NOT pay a bill. I would have to give him money if he needed it. It was my reality!

What type of "man" stops providing for his children and wife without an excuse of a layoff or getting sick? A male that does not care for himself and that became selfish in his thinking. BUT GOD, who cares for His people, continues to provide for them always. David says in his Psalms 37:25, "I have been young, and now am old; yet have I not seen the righteous forsaken, nor his seed begging bread." When I look up the meaning of "*forsaken*" its definition is "to leave alone or abandon."

If you know anything about David, he was called to do the work of the Lord at a very young age. If anyone can attest to this passage, it would be David. He had seen how God cared for him, even when he was not the "perfect saint."

God knew the calling on his life as well as what he was going to deal with to get to where He needed him to be.

If God knew us and what we were going to do before the foundation of the world, how in the world would he not honor what we need? It's us that push back our blessings because of lack of faith. Going through a time that I did not know where my next meal was going to come from, I found that the Lord put it on someone's heart to bless me. I remember a time I had just cooked the LAST of what I had for dinner. This time I didn't stress, "I just said Lord, it's on you! You know what we need." The next day a friend of mine texted me and said, "look under your mat, I left something under it." I go downstairs, and she leaves me a gift card to the local grocery store, and all I can do is cry and rejoice. The Lord knows what we need, and He cares enough for us to ensure we are taken care of, even if it's through someone else. Don't ever doubt God, because He will take care of you.

12 WHEN YOU OBEY GODS WORD

One of the biggest misconceptions and most debated topics I hear is regarding Tithing. I hear some say, "It was under the Law, it doesn't apply." I listen to others share "I didn't read it in the new testament." However, I wonder why is it such a big issue? Tithing was brought up before Moses gave the law. Genesis 14:17-20 "⁷ After Abram returned from defeating Kedorlaomer and the kings allied with him, the king of Sodom came out to meet him in the Valley of Shaveh (that is, the King's Valley).¹⁸ Then Melchizedek king of Salem brought out bread and wine. He was a priest of God Most High, ¹⁹ and he blessed Abram, saying, "Blessed be Abram by God Most High, Creator of heaven and earth.²⁰ And praise is to God Most High, who delivered your enemies into your hand. "Then Abram gave him a tenth of everything.

If this were done before the Law, this would be something to continue. You may be asking yourself, where does tithing come in with this book? Tithing has been what has kept food on the table, mortgage paid and never late with very LOW INCOME, a piece of mind, opportunities, and so many free items that I can't even name. But this was a promise from God. In Malachi 3:8-10, it says, "Will a man rob God? Ye have robbed me. But ye say Wherein have we robbed thee? In tithes and offerings.

9 Ye are cursed with a curse: for ye have robbed me, even this whole nation.

10 Bring ye all the tithes into the storehouse, that there may be meat in mine house, and prove me now herewith, saith the Lord of hosts, if I will not open you the windows of heaven, and pour you out a blessing, that there shall not be room enough to receive it.

People tend to mix "Alms" with "Tithes" without the proper understanding. Alms is something that you give to someone homeless or a charity; it is NOT to replace tithes.

Tithes are given to the "Storehouse" which is the house of the Lord. If a person ever finds themselves not wanting to give, that means they need to find where God wants them to be (I digress).

There was a specific time in life while married, I found that paying my household bills first and not taking care of God's business was more important. It seems like bills were piling up faster than I could pay them. I wanted to make sure our rent and bills were paid, so I stopped paying my tithes. I put my household before God, and that was not in order. During that time, I remember no matter how hard I tried, it seems like I continued to get deeper and deeper into debt. As a child, my mother taught my brothers and me the importance of paying tithe. I also watched how my mom continues to receive blessings upon blessings. However, for that moment (well few months) I had to put God's word aside and worry about my household.

I must say, that was the hardest time of my life. Even worse than not having money. The reason is that it seems like my money was decreasing as my bills were increasing. Eventually, I gave in and said, enough is enough. It's time to give back to God what is due Him. To this day, if I receive one dollar literally, ten cents will go into the offering with a smile. I robbed God, because I didn't trust him. I am supposed to lean on his promises, but I leaned on to my understanding at that moment. It was a lesson learned. My money was cursed, and I needed to break that curse. I see how the Lord did as He did at the wedding. If you recall, Jesus took two fish and five loaves and fed over 5000 men, women and children.

Why are we different? We are not. I've seen the Lord stretch my meals much longer than I expected. Remember, this is His promise. We must tell the Lord (as I often do) "I still have room to receive, LORD keep pouring out the blessings." Be faithful to paying your tithes. Give to a charity and those in need, but don't forget to separate the two—put God first. This may be the one thing that many may not agree with, but as I continue to see the promises of God I won't fight what He says in His word.

Being a divorced mother of three, I've watched how my obedience has allowed the Lord to fulfill his promises. I recently gave the last two dollars I had in my purse. I figured, what would I do with two dollars? Why not give it to the Lord and let him multiply it—and he did. I was blessed with much more than anticipated. You will be surprised at what God can do when you trust him and obey him.

13 ITS ALL IN THE PLAN

J eremiah 29:11, "For I know the thoughts that I think toward you, saith the Lord, the thoughts of peace and not evil, to give you an expected end." We tend to always look to man for how he/she sees us. Living in today's world, it's all about who sees us, who notices who we are, and what we are doing. Validation from someone seems to be desired much more from others than ever before.

Many people love "selfies." I recall being at an event asking someone if they wanted me to take a picture for them, and a woman said, "Oh no, I want to take a selfie." People know the perfect angle and what side would look better on camera. They seek "LIKES" on social media and often check as to how many people have watched their videos. But the question is, why does it matter? The Lord knows the thoughts He has towards you, and it's not about what man thinks, but what God thinks.

Marrying my ex-husband was not the best decision I made; however, it was in the plan. Before I was married, I was warned several times NOT to marry him from several people. I went into the office of my pastor, and he told me he couldn't marry me. Although disappointed, I wasn't upset. I knew that he had agreed under his oath he wouldn't marry someone unequally yoked. Yes, my ex-husband grew up in a Christian home, he didn't believe that speaking in tongues was necessary, and I did according to the word of God. (John 3:5, Acts 2:38-42). How can we walk together when we didn't agree, as discussed earlier in the book? We couldn't, because he wasn't a true believer.

I remember going to the altar for prayer the Sunday before we were set to get married. I asked the Lord to forgive me for I knew what I was doing and to "save" my "soon to be" husband so that we can live in a household of truth. But what I wasn't going to do is give up my dreams of being a wife and mother. I didn't want to lose out on marriage because I was the only one with crazy faith that believed that all things are possible. So, I married him—despite what others said. It was my life, my choice, and I had to live with the consequences. Although I did, I realized it was part of God's plan for me. NOT that He wanted me to get physically or emotionally abused, but since I made a choice, God continues to show me that He is with me. He gave me a way of escape and has provided for me through it all.

God is the one that will place the right spouse in your life, give you that perfect job, increase your finances, and help you become the person He intended for you to be. Do we see the God that we served, that He manifested Himself in the flesh (Jesus) (2 Timothy 3:16) and came down to earth, walked the earth and was beaten and died for our transgressions (sins)? We discredit who He is because the world has clouded our minds. It's the work of the enemy that has us not believing that God is who He is, and the enemy knows better than we do, but he is the author of confusion. He spent time with God in His presence and knows the truth.

We all have a purpose. Many of us have been prophesied to

regarding where God wants to take us, however, because it's not in the timing we are looking for, we push back and say, "it's taking too long." From there, we begin to move before God want us to move and find ourselves in a place in life we don't want to be. Our thoughts are not His thoughts, nor are our ways His (GOD) ways. We must understand that we cannot move forward without the blessings of God if we don't wait on Him.

God gives me peace that goes beyond my understanding. Philippians 4:7, "And the peace of God, which passeth all understanding, shall keep your hearts and minds through Christ Jesus." It's because of this peace that I have hope in God. He said in the word that we have an "expected" end. Why don't we live in expectation?

The Lord doesn't want evil to be done unto us. If I were to title my past marriage, it would be "Sleeping with the Enemy." I slept with a man that would fight me more than he would fight anyone else. I felt as if he wanted evil done to me and because he saw more in me than I saw in myself, he became jealous. His low self-esteem began to get weaker, and I would have to deal with his wrath. A husband is to be my protector and provider as I've mentioned earlier, not the enemy. But the God we serve says he has thoughts of peace and NOT evil.

I didn't have real peace in my home or life until recently. It was because I began to believe that the Lord has a great expected end for me. What I went through was part of my process to greater heights and deeper depths. As I draw closer to the Lord, I find myself opening more to what He wants from me. I find myself doing what the Lord asks of me, and I see His blessings upon my life every single day.

It's because of His promises; I continue to fall in love deeper and deeper with the God that I serve!

14 GOD WANTS THE BEST FOR ME

J ohn 3, 1-2 "Beloved, I wish above all things that thou mayest prosper and be in health even as thy soul prospers." Prosperity seems to be such a bad word among those that are saved and in the church. But for many, they are not studying the word of God. Prosperity is not just money. Psalms 1:3 says "and he shall be like a tree planted by the rivers of waters, that bringeth forth his fruit in his season, his leaf also shall not wither, and WHATSOEVER he doeth SHALL PROSPER."

This includes relationships with friends, the opposite sex in marriage, and on the job. When we get into relationships, we don't realize how much this can affect things around us and in us. If in 3 John he says, be in health. While being in my past marriage, I found that I was not in good mental health because of the things he would say and do to me. I often tell people how he changed my first name to the "B" word due to him calling me that more than anything. He didn't call me "baby," "honey," or any other cutesy name that people that love their spouse call them. Other than that, I was just Kama. During the ending of our marriage he tried a few times, but it did not seem like it was right. It felt weird because it wasn't something I was used to hearing from him. One day he was home from his rendezvous, and I decided to go through his phone. Please note, in the many years we had been together, I didn't believe in going into anyone's pager or phone for that matter. This time I just needed the proof that he continued to lie to me about. Evidence that he had a girlfriend. He was in the restroom, and I reached over and looked at his phone, and the first message to her was "BABE, pick up some trees (marijuana)." I thought what the heck, did he call her baby and I'm the 4-legged female dog? I immediately knew that I was DONE at that point.

I remember dating a guy, and he started to call me "baby" and "My Luv" and it felt right. It made me feel like he meant it. Although we didn't last, there was something about it coming from someone that I knew cared—at that time at least.

The names that I was called hurt me so badly; it penetrated my heart and my soul to the point that I believed that is who I was at the time. My ex-husband called me a "hoe" because I had males on my Facebook page. He accused me of being with all these guys because he didn't know the males that were on my page. I explained that I have men on my page I've known since elementary school, church, and people I've met over the years, but he said there is no way. For a woman that had only been with one man (which was him) it had me looking at and questioning myself. It may sound strange. However, he taunted me with it. Mental health is just as important as physical health, because it brings on stress, and stress brings problems such as ulcers and tension.

In 2015, I went through a very rough time with my health. I read, when people deal with Domestic Violence, one of the lasting effects is muscle tension. I dealt with that, and it was no joke. But this is not what was intended by God. His word says that we be in health. Following and obeying

God's word, His voice will keep you in good health and help you as you make the decisions about who is going to work side by side with you in a relationship.

When we are planted in God and not wavering and double-minded, the word of God says, "...and whatsoever he doeth shall prosper." But we must be like a tree planted by the rivers of water that bringeth forth fruit. What are you bearing for this promise to be fulfilled? God has given all of us a purpose on this earth. People tend to say, "I don't have talents," "I just don't have it." But there is no excuse as to why you can't dig deeper into what you love to do, and it can glorify our Lord and Savior, our God Jesus Christ. I'm no different than anyone else.

For me, I wish I could sing. It seems like just about everyone that is around me can sing or hold a note and it's just not in me. The Lord gave me a different gift, something I've been working in since I was a child and didn't realize it until I became an adult. The Lord uses me to inspire others around. Through my life, my words and my giving of myself unselfishly, I find myself prospering in everything I touch. Times get hard and even the process, but because I am rooted and grounded, through my struggles, God still sustains me, and I again prosper. Therefore, I continue to follow God's word.

My story of abuse is not a story of "WOE IS ME." It's a story of strength in the time of a storm; it's a story of perseverance and account of what God's plans are for me. If I didn't go through any of what I dealt with, I don't know where my life would be. BUT God, in my disobedience, still had a plan for my life!

15 CONCLUSION

Falling in love with the promises of God will get you to the point that you will learn more about you. I hear women focus on having a man in their life and they end up with one that they did not expect. Such as an abusive man, a cheater, and a man that is after her money. The reason for this is because as females, I don't know too many that want to be alone. I hear women make statements such as "I will never get married again." But I think to myself, do you feel that way? Is that the bitterness talking? OR is that because men are not knocking on your door every day.

What I have learned about falling in love with God's promises is that I have learned how to truly love me first! The Lord has a way of showing you who you are if you are willing to keep your eyes and hearts open to the true you. When you are focusing on the "true you" you will find out things about yourself that need to be corrected. Maybe it's your attitude towards others or men because of past hurts. You know they say, "Hurt people, HURT people." It could be that you need to take time and focus on your finances and credit. Maybe it is the fact that you haven't spent enough time with your children due to other people in your pathway. It also could be the Lord wanting you to spend more time with Him to get into His presence so that you can recognize what you truly have in Him. If you begin to draw closer to the Lord and focus on what God has for you, He would start to mold you into the best WIFE as possible, and you will be able to recognize the man He wants you to be with.

We are to marry ONE man, not many. We are to focus on our children (if we have any), ourselves, and not worry about everyone else—UNLESS God says otherwise. Remember that God's promises are Yea and Amen. There is no way He can go back on His word. Don't forget, "God is not a man, that he should lie; neither the son of man, that he should repent: hath he said, and shall he not do it? or hath he spoken, and shall he not make it good?" (Numbers 23:19). If God tells you something, stand on His word. It can never fail you.

I'm sure as you read this book you began to think of promises that were made to you by someone. It may have brought up old memories, some regret, and maybe even some hurt. But it is time to empty yourself of the hurt and pain, and begin to reach out to the Lord and ask Him to mend your broken heart. The last few pages of this book serve as a space that will allow you to journal your promises from the Lord and begin to make promises to yourself that you want in life.

If it is a spouse, declare the type of person you are asking the Lord for in your life. If it is a career, financial goal, family goal, or weight goal, write it down and pray and fast over it. Then give it to the Lord entirely and do NOT stress over it. The word says, "Be careful with nothing; but in everything by prayer and supplication with thanksgiving, let your requests be made known unto God" (Philippians 4:6).

You will be surprised how fast God works when it's written down. If someone prophecies to you, record it, or have someone record and write it in this book with the date. It is the way God is confirming to you that He hears you. "And the LORD answered me, and said, Write the vision, and make it plain upon tables, that he may run that readeth it. For the vision is yet for an appointed time, but at the end, it shall speak, and not lie though it tarry, wait for it; because it will surely come, it will not tarry." Habakkuk 2:2-3

Psalms 37:4 says to Delight thyself in the Lord, and He will give you the promises of your heart! Don't fall in love with man and his promises, but fall in love with the promises of God!

-End-

ABOUT THE AUTHOR

Kama Burton, mother of 3, REALTOR® (14 years), Founder of Loving Me 1st (nonprofit), creator of Girls Club, Speaker, Trainer, and Coach. Kama was in a 12-year marriage (total) that took a turn for the worse. She dealt with every aspect of Domestic Violence. At one point, she didn't feel like she was good enough to prosper in too much in life. It took many people to see more in her than she could see in herself. During that time of marriage, Kama managed to go to school, become a REALTOR® to be able to stay at home and still make ends meet. She also obtained her Associates of Science Degree from Riverside Community college, where she is now a Professor teaching Real Estate Courses to help others achieve their Real Estate License, and she completed the University of Phoenix where she obtained her bachelor's degree in Business Management. Although she was going through a rough time in life, Kama fought through it and never gave up. Kama started a Girls Club teaching our girls to Love and know who they are first. She is in a local School District teaching girl from 5th grade to 12th grade. Her passion is to ensure the girls don't get into toxic relationships and help them become skilled leaders in the community. Kama has the heart to help those that are seeking to Pursue their passion. She started a talk show called "Kama Speaks" (formally Pursuing Your Passion) on YouTube in 2013 where she interviewed over 100 entrepreneurs that didn't allow obstacles to get into the way of their purpose. She just began the show again as she is building her Coaching platform to help REALTORS® through Coach Ella Blaine and other Entrepreneurs go after their goals through John Maxwell's Coaching and Training. Kama is a speaker who as spoke to thousands throughout the year regarding Real Estate, pursuing their passion and her story.

To book Kama Burton,
Speaker, Trainer, Coaching, and Workshop Facilitator
Please email Kama@kamaspeaks.com

Journal

_____

_____

_____

_____

_____

_____

_____

_____

_____

_____

_____

_____

_____

_____

_____

_____

_____

_____

_____

_____

_____

_____

Journal

_____

_____

_____

_____

_____

_____

_____

_____

_____

_____

_____

_____

_____

_____

_____

_____

_____

_____

_____

_____

_____

_____

_____

_____

_____

_____

Journal

_____

_____

_____

_____

_____

_____

_____

_____

_____

_____

_____

_____

_____

_____

_____

_____

_____

_____

_____

_____

_____

_____

_____

Made in the USA
Monee, IL
29 September 2023

43662961R00059